I0797322

The Kite Runner

Lightbox Literature Studies

Blaine Wiseman and Katie Gillespie

LIGHTBOX
openlightbox.com

LIGHTBOX

Go to
www.openlightbox.com
and enter this book's
unique code.

ACCESS CODE

LBXD6665

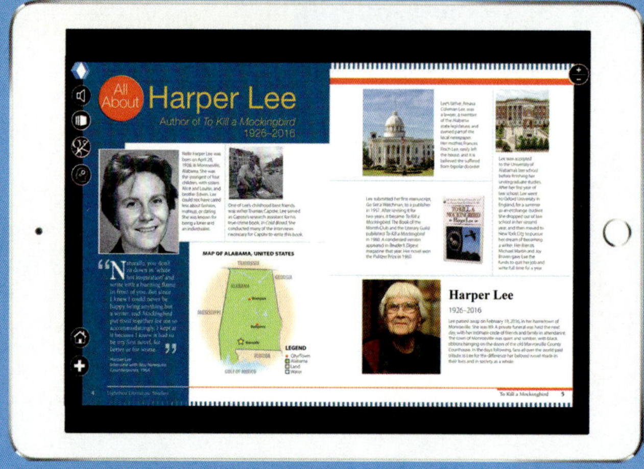

Lightbox is an all-inclusive digital solution for the teaching and learning of curriculum topics in an original, groundbreaking way. Lightbox is based on National Curriculum Standards.

STANDARD FEATURES OF LIGHTBOX

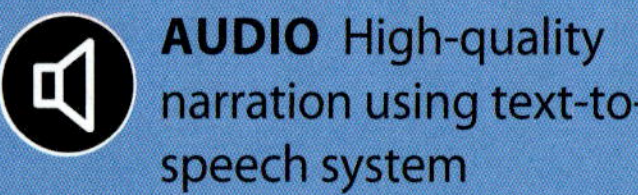

AUDIO High-quality narration using text-to-speech system

VIDEOS Embedded high-definition video clips

ACTIVITIES Printable PDFs that can be emailed and graded

WEBLINKS Curated links to external, child-safe resources

SLIDESHOWS Pictorial overviews of key concepts

TRANSPARENCIES Step-by-step layering of maps, diagrams, charts, and timelines

INTERACTIVE MAPS Interactive maps and aerial satellite imagery

QUIZZES Ten multiple choice questions that are automatically graded and emailed for teacher assessment

KEY WORDS Matching key concepts to their definitions

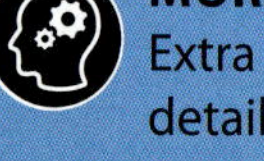

MORE Extra information and details on the subject

FIRST HAND Letters, diaries, and other primary sources

DOCS Speeches, newspaper articles, and other historical documents

Contents

'Unforgettable ... extraordinary. It is so powerful that for a long time after, everything I read seemed bland'
ISABEL ALLENDE
'Shattering ... devastating and inspiring'
OBSERVER
The Kite Runner
KHALED HOSSEINI

RUBRIC

Conducting an Interview

Students will conduct an interview with a community member about a time period in their community's history, and submit an audio recording and transcript of the interview. An exemplary interview will meet the following criteria.

- Clearly defines the purpose of the interview
- Conducts thorough background research to inform the focus of the interview and the questions
- Drafts a complete list of thoughtful, in-depth, and varied questions prior to the interview
- Interviews a subject with relevant knowledge on the topic and time period in question
- Asks questions in a logical order, building upon each other
- Treats the interview subject in a polite, respectful, and professional manner
- Does not interrupt or rush the interview subject
- Shows interest and enthusiasm in responses and follow-up questions
- Chooses follow-up questions that demonstrate active listening
- Asks for clarification and further details when necessary
- Asks questions about personal experiences related to the topic
- Asks questions regarding factual information and the interview subject's opinion on the topic
- Asks creative questions that reflect fresh insights on the topic
- Records the full interview in a quiet environment
- Organizes and edits the interview transcript to be clear and factual

Khaled Hosseini

Author of *The Kite Runner*

1965–

Khaled Hosseini has become one of the most successful, celebrated, and well-known authors of the twenty-first century. He found instant success with his debut novel, *The Kite Runner*, in 2003. Since then, Hosseini has written two more critically acclaimed, best-selling novels. In 2007, *A Thousand Splendid Suns* spent its first fifteen weeks after publication at number one on *The New York Times* bestseller list. *And the Mountains Echoed*, Hosseini's third novel, was published in 2013, selling three million copies in its first five months. Hosseini's books feature epic storytelling, spanning decades and continents. Inspiration for the settings and events in his stories is often autobiographical, drawing on the author's life experiences.

> **"A complete community needs people who work with their hands, and people who work with their minds. It demands an older generation that's had years of experience, and new blood to bring about innovation. It must have people who are cautious, and people who are bold. It needs women and men. It needs loyalists and also critics. A community must recognize, want, and care for its own. Sometimes the people who need the most help are the hardest to see."**
>
> Khaled Hosseini, Commencement speech at Vanderbilt University, 2010

MAP OF THE WORLD

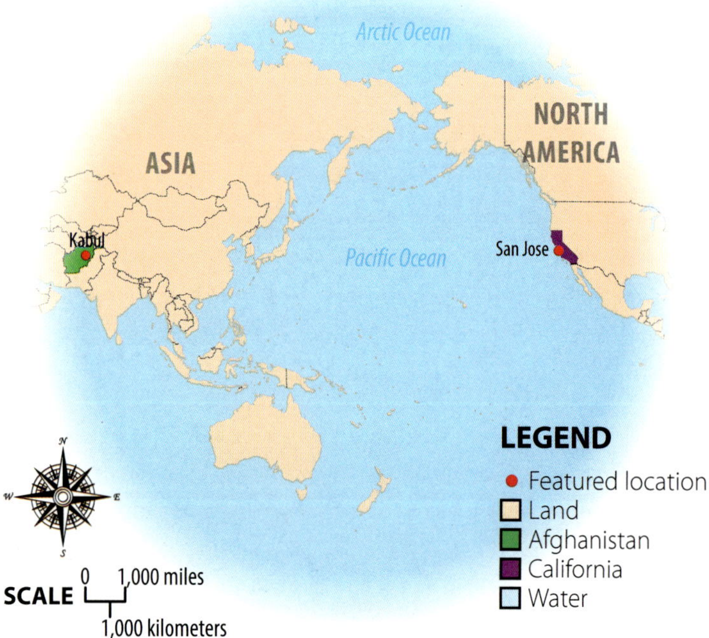

Hosseini was born on March 4, 1965, in Kabul, Afghanistan, a city featured heavily in his works. He grew up in a peaceful, progressive Afghanistan, with four younger brothers and sisters. Their father was a **diplomat**, and their mother a high school teacher of **Farsi** and history. Hosseini spent his free time reading and writing stories, watching American movies, and flying kites with friends.

Hosseini worked hard to learn English while his parents supported the family. In 1984, he graduated from high school and continued his education, pursuing a career in medicine. Beginning with a bachelor's degree in biology from Santa Clara University, Hosseini then moved on to medical school at the University of California, San Diego. About 13 years after arriving in America, he earned his medical degree, and spent the following three years completing his residency.

In 1976, the family moved to Paris, France, where Hosseini's father was given a job with the Foreign Ministry. His posting ended in 1980, and the Hosseini family was ready to return home. Two years prior, however, a Communist **coup** drove Afghanistan into political turmoil and war. It had become unsafe to return home, so the family applied for political asylum in the United States. They became part of a growing Afghan **diaspora** in America, settling in San Jose, California.

In 1997, Hosseini began writing a short story called *The Kite Runner*, which was rejected by several literary magazines. After returning to northern California in 1999, he kept writing in his spare time. Finally, in 2003, *The Kite Runner* had become a full-length novel, and was published by Riverhead Books. Today, Hosseini has been granted an open-ended **sabbatical** from practicing medicine in order to pursue his writing career. He also works for **non-profit** organizations such as the United Nations Refugee Agency (UNHCR). His books have entertained millions of people around the world and spread awareness about the plight of people living in Afghanistan.

ACTIVITIES

Google Maps

Kabul, Afghanistan

Explore Khaled Hosseini's birthplace, using street view. The city of Kabul is also the setting of *The Kite Runner*.

First Hand

'Kite Runner' Author On His Childhood, His Writing, And The Plight Of Afghan Refugees

Examine this interview with Khaled Hosseini from *RadioFreeEurope RadioLiberty*.

1. What types of questions does the interviewer ask? What topics are discussed the most? Why do you think the focus is on these specific areas?
2. The interviewer asks Hosseini to describe the impact that 30 years of war has had on his country's culture, and on the daily life of Afghans. How does his response reflect the experiences of the characters he has created? Why do you think this is the case? What effect has the war had on the way these characters are portrayed?

RUBRIC

Researching for a Writing Assignment

Students will complete a thorough research process to prepare for a writing assignment, and organize their research in a logical manner that supports their writing. An exemplary research process will meet the following criteria.

- Creates a goal for the research, based on the topic and working thesis
- Creates specific, thoughtful, and inventive research questions that are relevant to the topic of the writing assignment
- Produces a list of categories, key words, and related ideas to effectively assist in researching
- Uses high-quality sources that pertain to the topic and come in a variety of formats, such as books, journals, primary sources, websites, and databases
- Determines accuracy of all sources
- Uses sources that provide balanced research and various perspectives on the topic in question
- Takes notes to highlight the key facts and ideas in order to answer all research questions
- Extracts relevant, detailed information from the sources during the note-taking process
- Organizes the research notes in a clear and concise manner
- Organizes the research notes logically and in a way that sets up the information and ideas for analysis and the writing process
- Analyzes the information and produces ideas and points to support the working thesis
- Uses an effective and suitable format to present all research
- Properly cites all sources used

Setting of the Novel

Setting plays an important role in *The Kite Runner*, as Amir's descriptions of places reflect the changes that he, his people, and his country undergo. A hometown filled with happiness and love begins to deteriorate, forcing a relocation to a foreign land where Amir and Baba strive to keep hold of their roots. From a peaceful childhood in Kabul to a tumultuous adolescence in the United States, Amir returns to the war-ravaged Kabul as a man. Upon his return, Amir finds his former home as damaged as his soul.

Snapshot

Kabul is Afghanistan's **largest city**, with an estimated population of more than **3 million residents**.

Each year from **1980** to **1989**, between **2,000 and 4,000** Afghans moved to the United States.

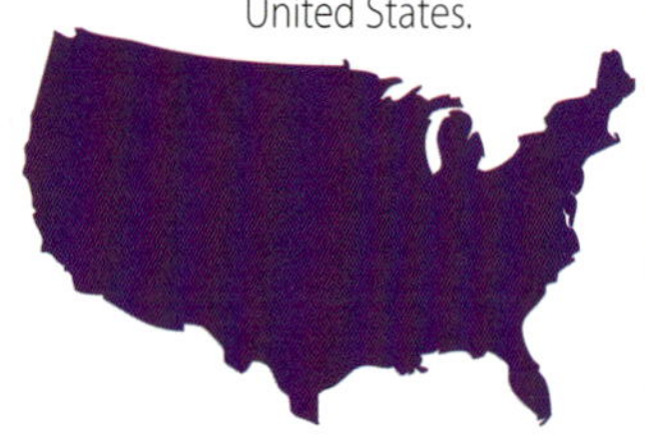

It is estimated that about **60 percent** of Afghan refugees **in the United States** live in the **San Francisco Bay area**.

Back to Baba's House

"The driveway extension that led from the gates to the yard, where Hassan and I took turns falling the summer we learned to ride a bike, didn't look as wide or as long as I remembered it. The asphalt had split in a lightning-streak pattern, and more tangles of weed sprouted through the fissures. Most of the poplar trees had been chopped down—the trees Hassan and I used to climb to shine our mirrors into the neighbors' homes. The ones still standing were nearly leafless. The Wall of Ailing Corn was still there, though I saw no corn, ailing or otherwise, along that wall now. The paint had begun to peel and sections of it had sloughed off altogether."

Amir, Chapter twenty-one

From Baba's Kabul home to the San Jose flea market, the settings in *The Kite Runner* are described through a uniquely Afghan viewpoint. The streets of Wazir Akbar Khan serve as Amir and Hassan's kite fighting colosseum, and the hill behind Baba's house is where they crown themselves the Sultans of Kabul. Later, in the United States, Baba, Amir, and the rest of their Afghan community try to recreate an authentic Afghan experience. At the flea market in San Jose, the Afghan merchants gather for tea, kolcha, gossip, and stories of past glory. Amir and Soraya's wedding brings the community together, celebrating their love in traditional Afghan style.

Many of the settings featured in *The Kite Runner* reflect those most important in the life of the author. Scenes set in California depict the author's, and the narrator's, efforts to build a new life in a new land. Amir's desire to lead a normal American life reflects how Hosseini likely felt during his adolescence in California. Despite these desires, he can never forget Afghanistan, and longs for his homeland. The most vivid stories and imagery in the novel appear in Afghanistan, most notably in the city of Kabul, the city of Amir's and also of Hosseini's childhood. It is the place where Amir finally returns to face his **reckoning**.

ACTIVITIES

Video

Historical and Political Context for "The Kite Runner"

Find out more about the historical and political context of *The Kite Runner* by watching this video.

1. Why was Afghanistan chosen as the setting for this story? Could the novel have been set anywhere else? Why or why not?
2. In the video, it is mentioned that the film adaptation of *The Kite Runner* shows women not wearing burqas. Why do you think this is significant? How might viewers in Afghanistan and in the United States perceive this?

Weblink

Afghanistan on intimate scale in 'The Kite Runner'

Learn more about Hosseini's presentation of Afghanistan in the novel by reading this article.

1. It is noted in the article that Hosseini "began life as a privileged young Afghan." In what ways might his personal experiences growing up have affected the way Hosseini characterizes Amir, and his relationship with Hassan? Support your answer with evidence from the novel.
2. Although Hosseini says that he "fully recognize[s] the challenges Afghanistan faces," he also asserts that "at the same time, things have improved." Do you believe that he is correct? Why or why not? What parallels can you draw between Hosseini's claim and the events of the novel?

Time Period of the Novel

The Kite Runner is spread over a time period spanning decades, from the 1960s, when Amir and Hassan are children in Kabul, to the story's culmination in the early 2000s, when Amir brings Sohrab to America. The story progresses against a backdrop of change in Afghanistan and its effect on the lives of the country's people. Time period and setting share an important link in *The Kite Runner*, as Amir's present is constantly driven by his past.

Change in Afghanistan

"Rubble and beggars. Everywhere I looked, that was what I saw. I remembered beggars in the old days too—Baba always carried an extra handful of Afghani bills in his pocket just for them; I'd never seen him deny a peddler. Now, though, they squatted at every street corner, dressed in shredded burlap rags, mud-caked hands held out for a coin. And the beggars were mostly children now, thin and grim-faced, some no older than five or six. They sat in the laps of their *burqa*-clad mothers alongside gutters at busy street corners and chanted, '*Bakhshesh, bakhshesh*!' And something else, something I hadn't noticed right away: Hardly any of them sat with an adult male—the wars had made fathers a rare commodity in Afghanistan."

Amir, Chapter twenty

Amir

The early chapters of *The Kite Runner* are set in a peaceful, prosperous Kabul, a city where Amir and Hassan, two boys from different backgrounds, are free to grow together. As the story progresses, however, growing religious and political tension play a major role in tearing the two companions apart. Life goes on for both, but they endure great suffering in the subsequent years. Amir and Baba suffer the hardship and humiliation experienced by millions of Afghan refugees beginning in the 1970s, which Hosseini also experienced firsthand. Amir is haunted by the memory of Hassan, who is left behind in Afghanistan. The terrible fate suffered by Hassan is one shared by millions of victims of Afghanistan's decades of war and unrest.

The Afghanistan of Amir and Hassan's childhood is a mix of ancient and contemporary. Amir describes the giant Buddha statues in Bamiyan, which were subsequently and notoriously destroyed, and going to the cinema to see a new Afghan film, a pastime that would soon become impossible. The Kabul of his childhood is a contemporary place, where Baba is free to drive his Ford Mustang, and Amir and Hassan watch American movies starring John Wayne and Clint Eastwood, while drinking Coca-Cola. War is a thing of the past, as old Russian tanks rust on the side of the highway.

Communism is gone, capitalism reigns, and religion is a major part of life, but **secularism** is completely acceptable. Underneath the surface, however, **fundamentalism** is growing, and communism is making a comeback. The peace of Amir and Hassan's childhood is under threat from forces inside and outside Afghanistan. The drama and hardship that soon face Amir and Hassan begin with an eruption of gunfire in the streets in 1973. A military coup overthrows the king, brings international forces back into play, and raises religious tensions. When the Soviet Union intervenes in 1979, all hope of peace is lost. In the next decade, more than a million Afghan civilians would be killed, and millions more would be forced to flee the country.

ACTIVITIES

Video

Feature History - Soviet-Afghan War

Discover more about the time period of *The Kite Runner* by watching this video.

1. Although *The Kite Runner* is a work of fiction, it does draw on real-life events. As noted in the video, due to the Soviet-Afghan War, "millions of Afghans died and even more still live as refugees." How does knowing this affect your perception of the characters in the novel? What parallels can be drawn between the fictional story of Amir and Hassan, and actual events experienced by millions of people?
2. How did the time period that *The Kite Runner* was written in impact Hosseini's creation of the novel? In what ways might the story be different if it were written today?

Weblink

The History of Afghanistan during the Time of The Kite Runner

Learn about the historical events that Hosseini drew on when writing *The Kite Runner*.

1. In the article, it is noted that Amir's story demonstrates "a frightening time for the people of Kabul who heard rioting and shooting in the streets." Why do you think Hosseini chooses to depict these real-life events from Amir's perspective? Is this an effective way to connect with readers? Why or why not?
2. As explained in the article, the novel shows "how the Taliban used fear and violence to control the people of Afghanistan." Why was this an effective method? Give specific examples.

RUBRIC

Writing a Short Story

Students will choose an excerpt from the novel and use it as their inspiration in writing a short story. An exemplary short story will meet the following criteria.

- Engages the reader from the opening line
- Establishes a clear, consistent point of view
- Introduces a narrator and a setting
- Develops an engaging conflict at the heart of the narrative to build tension and keep the reader interested
- Develops characters and events through purposeful and well-crafted literary devices
- Creates a logical progression of events in the narrative that build upon each other using various techniques
- Explores ideas, concepts, and writing styles with creativity and originality
- Demonstrates a high level of skill in using appropriate narrative techniques to tell the story
- Concludes the narrative in a thoughtful, effective manner appropriate to the narrative
- Uses varied, purposeful diction and syntax to affect style and serve the narrative
- Writes with clarity, imagination, and a unique, personal voice
- Does not use stereotypes or clichés
- Uses effective, believable dialogue
- Uses correct spelling, grammar, and punctuation

Conflict in the Novel

Conflict has reigned in Afghanistan for four decades. It is no surprise then, that *The Kite Runner* is a book filled with conflict. Major conflicts involving international powers, monarchs and governments, and political and religious **factions** drive the book's storyline. Smaller interpersonal and internal conflicts, however, create the greatest turmoil for the characters.

The Four Major Types of Conflict in Literature

MAN vs. MAN

Sara Gruen's *Water for Elephants* tells the story of Jacob Jankowski, a young man who joins a traveling circus, looking for a new life. He finds a difficult existence working for the evil Uncle Al and the abusive animal trainer, August. Jacob's love for August's wife, Marlena, and his respect for the intelligent elephant, Rosie, bring him into conflict with his bosses.

MAN vs. SELF

Some works of literature resonate with readers because they capture the internal struggles inherent in human nature. In *The Fault in Our Stars* by John Green, Hazel Grace Lancaster is a teenage girl battling **terminal** cancer. Hazel's struggle to accept her **prognosis**, and later, that of the boy she loves, form the basis of this touching story.

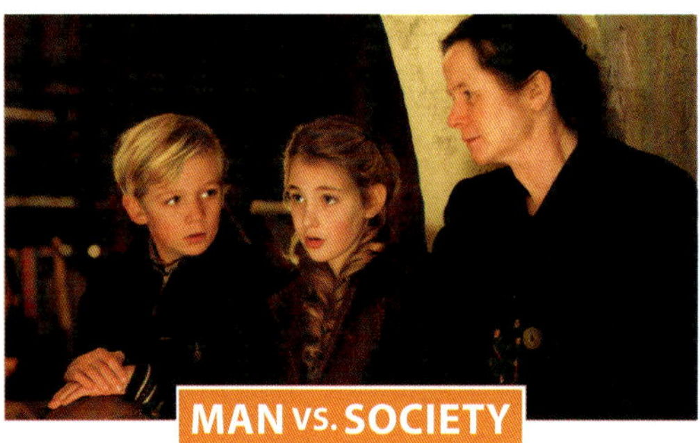

MAN vs. SOCIETY

Markus Zusak's *The Book Thief* takes place in Germany during World War II. Characters living in the midst of war often find themselves in conflict with society. *The Book Thief* features a young orphan named Liesel, whose adopted family shelters a Jewish man from the Nazi regime. This puts them in conflict with the Nazi government, led by Adolf Hitler, as well as their friends and neighbors who are sympathetic to the Nazis.

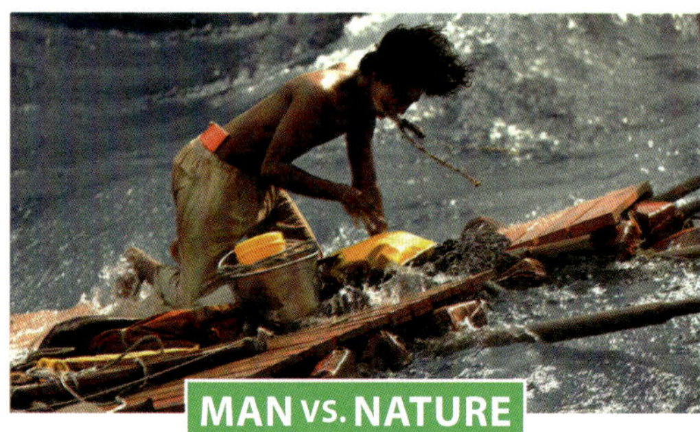

MAN vs. NATURE

Literary history is filled with tales of shipwrecked sailors lost at sea. A modern example of such a story is Yann Martel's *Life of Pi*. In this modern classic, the protagonist, Pi, spends a large portion of the book stranded in a life boat. Not only must Pi battle the burning Sun, fierce wind and rains, swelling seas, thirst, and hunger, he must also face his companion in the boat, a full-grown Bengal tiger.

Types of Conflict in *The Kite Runner*

Man versus Society

"I never thought of Hassan and me as friends...Not in the usual sense, anyhow...Never mind that we spent entire winters flying kites, running kites. Never mind that to me, the face of Afghanistan is that of a boy with a thin-boned frame, a shaved head, and low-set ears, a boy with a Chinese doll face perpetually lit by a hare-lipped smile. Never mind any of those things. Because history isn't easy to overcome. Neither is religion. In the end, I was a Pashtun and he was a Hazara, I was Sunni and he was a Shi'a, and nothing was ever going to change that. Nothing."

Amir, Chapter four

Man versus Man

"'I've been wondering,' the Talib said, his bloodshot eyes peering at me over Sohrab's shoulder. 'Whatever happened to old *Babalu*, anyway?'...He laughed. 'What did you think? That you'd put on a fake beard and I wouldn't recognize you? Here's something I'll bet you never knew about me: I never forget a face. Not ever.' He brushed his lips against Sohrab's ear, kept his eye on me. 'I heard your father died. *Tsk-tsk*. I always did want to take him on. Looks like I'll have to settle for his weakling of a son.'"

Amlr, Chapter twenty-two

Man versus Nature

"When the tests were over, he explained that he couldn't explain why we couldn't have kids. And, apparently, that wasn't so unusual. It was called 'Unexplained Infertility.'"

Amir, Chapter thirteen

Man versus Self

"I became what I am today at the age of twelve, on a frigid overcast day in the winter of 1975...That was a long time ago, but it's wrong what they say about the past, I've learned, about how you can bury it. Because the past claws its way out. Looking back now, I realize I have been peeking into that deserted alley for the last twenty-six years."

Amir, Chapter one

ACTIVITIES

More

The Types of Conflict in *The Kite Runner*

Analyze the excerpts from the novel revealing the types of conflict as they appear in *The Kite Runner*.

1. How do these excerpts of conflict reveal the novel's theme? How do they reveal character? Explain and defend your ideas.
2. Write an analysis of Hosseini's development of conflict between Amir and Assef. What deeper truths may be suggested about these characters as a result of their conflict?

Document

The Kite Runner and the Problem of Racism and Ethnicity

Review the essay by Akram Sadat Hosseini and Esmaeil Zohdi of Vali-e-Asr University, exploring the novel.

1. Who do you think is the intended audience for this document? Why? Are the tone and language used appropriate for this audience? Explain your answer.
2. What are the main points of the document and how are they presented? Are these points conveyed effectively to the reader? Why or why not?

RUBRIC

Holding a Classroom Debate

Students will form groups and prepare arguments for a debate on a controversial issue. Exemplary performance in a debate will meet the following criteria.

- Demonstrates in-depth understanding of the topic and related information
- Presents strong, logical, and convincing arguments
- Communicates in a clear and confident manner
- Maintains eye contact
- Uses clear vocal tone and a reasonable rate of vocal delivery
- Uses respectful and appropriate language and body language
- Delivers arguments, evidence, and counter-evidence in an engaging and persuasive manner
- Supports each major point of an argument with several relevant and detailed facts and examples
- Connects all arguments to the overall topic in a clear, concise, and organized manner
- Presents the arguments and supporting evidence in a clear, logical manner
- Presents clear, thorough, and accurate information throughout the debate
- Addresses all of the opposing team's arguments with counter-arguments
- Identifies any weakness in the opposing team's arguments
- Constructs strong and relevant counter-arguments using accurate information
- Presents strong and persuasive arguments throughout the debate
- Summarizes the arguments in the closing statement

Introducing the Characters

Memorable characters are central to any story. Readers are engaged by their struggles and triumphs, conflicts and relationships, and changes and growth. *The Kite Runner*'s characters are human—they have faults, flaws, doubts, and anxieties. They also make mistakes, learn important lessons, and adapt accordingly. These types of characters can inspire readers to adapt to their own surroundings. Hosseini used real life as his inspiration to create characters who turn weakness into strength, fear into courage, and despair into hope.

Major Characters in *The Kite Runner*

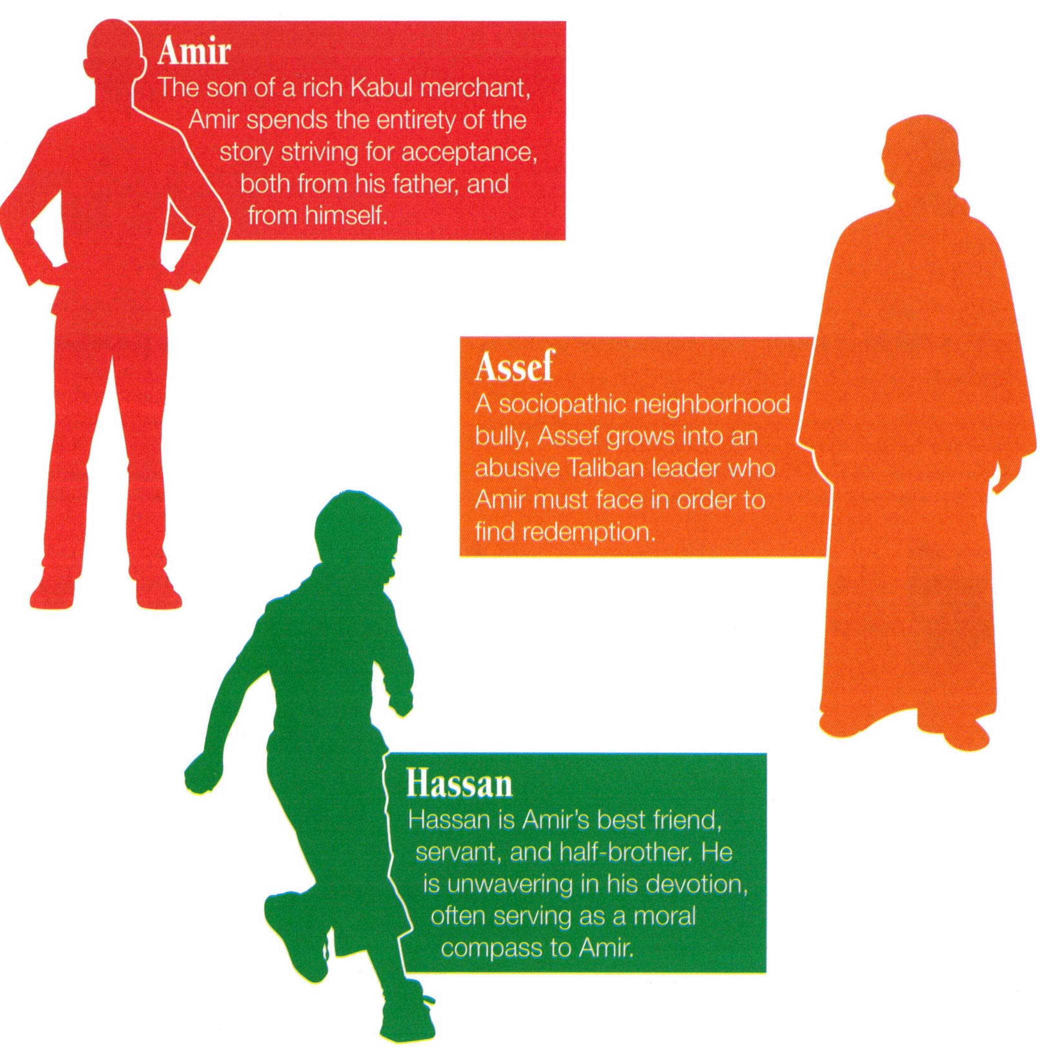

Amir, who is both the protagonist and the narrator, recounts the story from his perspective as an adult. He is driven to atone for the wrongs he committed against his friend and half-brother, Hassan. From early on, Amir describes their relationship as unequal. Hassan is a dedicated, helpful, protective, and unselfish friend and servant, but Amir manipulates Hassan for his own entertainment and gain. This behavior leads to, and is reinforced by, the central incident in the story, when Amir fails to protect Hassan, and then turns against him.

As the narrator, Amir gives readers a deep, **introspective** view of his **psyche**. His fears, doubts, regrets, hopes, and aspirations are laid bare, and the reader learns about Amir through his most intimate thoughts and feelings, along with his actions. As Amir grows and changes throughout the book, so do his priorities, desires, and attitude. Amir is a dynamic character, and his observations serve to introduce the rest of the book's characters as well. His selective memories and observations shape the way readers view the story's supporting cast.

Baba is also a dynamic character. At times, Amir views Baba as an inspirational, saint-like figure of great strength. At other times, Baba is portrayed as stubborn, confrontational, judgmental, ignorant, weak, and proud. These observations reflect Amir as a character as much as they do Baba. Hassan is a static character who represents all that is good in Amir's world. He is always ready to stand up for what is right and enjoys the simple joys of life, views that never change. Assef, however, is a one-dimensional, evil representation of a static character. From the early chapters to the final confrontation with Amir, Assef only grows more sadistic.

Baba
Amir's father is a towering, masculine, successful, well-respected merchant who strives to instill the same qualities in his reluctant son.

Ali
Ali is Hassan's father, and Baba's lifelong companion and servant. Although he is crippled and disfigured, Ali is a gentle, patient, and kind guardian to both Hassan and Amir.

Rahim Khan
Baba's best friend and business partner is an understanding and encouraging presence in Amir's life.

Soraya
Soraya is the daughter of an acquaintance of Baba's in California. Despite their troubled pasts, Soraya and Amir fall in love and get married.

Sohrab
Sohrab is Hassan's son, orphaned by the war, and abused by Assef and his Taliban comrades. He represents Amir's chance at redemption.

ACTIVITIES

Weblink

Character Analysis of Amir

Review a character analysis of Amir and debate his role in *The Kite Runner*.

1. When Hassan is being assaulted by Assef, Amir simply watches. Why do you think Amir does not intervene to help Hassan? How does this affect the reader's opinion of him? Give textual evidence to support your claims.
2. It is suggested that it "takes Amir thirty years to redeem himself, and even then we're not entirely sure it's enough." Do you believe this kind of redemption is possible, and if so, has Amir redeemed himself by the end of the novel? If not, why do you think this is not possible, and what effect does this have on Amir?

More

Character Development in *The Kite Runner*

Analyze the characters in *The Kite Runner* using the descriptions on the character map and excerpts from each character. Then, choose a character and answer the following questions.

1. Which of the writer's techniques are most effective at revealing this character's traits? Why?
2. In what ways is the characterization of this character ineffective? What could be done to improve this character's function in the novel? Defend your ideas with evidence.

RUBRIC

Creating a Literary Device Analysis Booklet

Students will analyze the author's use of a literary device in the novel, and create a booklet to present this analysis. An exemplary literary device analysis booklet will meet the following criteria.

- Defines the chosen literary device accurately and in detail
- Places the definition of the literary device at the beginning of the booklet
- Provides strong, specific examples of how this literary device is used in the novel
- Describes examples in detail, with quotations properly integrated
- Includes thorough analysis of the use, purpose, and effectiveness of each example of how the chosen literary device is used in the novel
- Arranges all pages logically
- Examples are organized chronologically
- Provides no more than one example and its analysis per page
- Creates a neat, well-organized, and attractive booklet
- Booklet is colorful and displays the student's creativity
- Uses illustrations to represent the chosen literary device and the examples of how it is used in the novel

The Art of Storytelling

The Kite Runner is a story filled with symbolism. It uses changing settings to frame the characters' experiences. The mood and tone of the story swing from positive to negative, happy to tragic, and dreadful to hopeful. Each chapter, interaction, and event advances the story toward its culmination. Hosseini's use of literary elements and techniques draws the reader in, creating a mix of emotions, and a dramatic, intriguing story that engages readers.

Structure of a Narrative

While *The Kite Runner* makes excellent use of flashbacks and memories to create context, it follows a simple, common narrative structure. For the most part, the story advances in a **chronological** timeline with a defined beginning, middle, and end. It begins with Amir's childhood in Kabul, where his entire world changes. The middle of the story features Amir's attempts to move on in America, forgetting his past and creating a happier future for himself. The end, however, brings him back to his past and forces him to deal with the demons he has carried with him.

Freytag's Pyramid

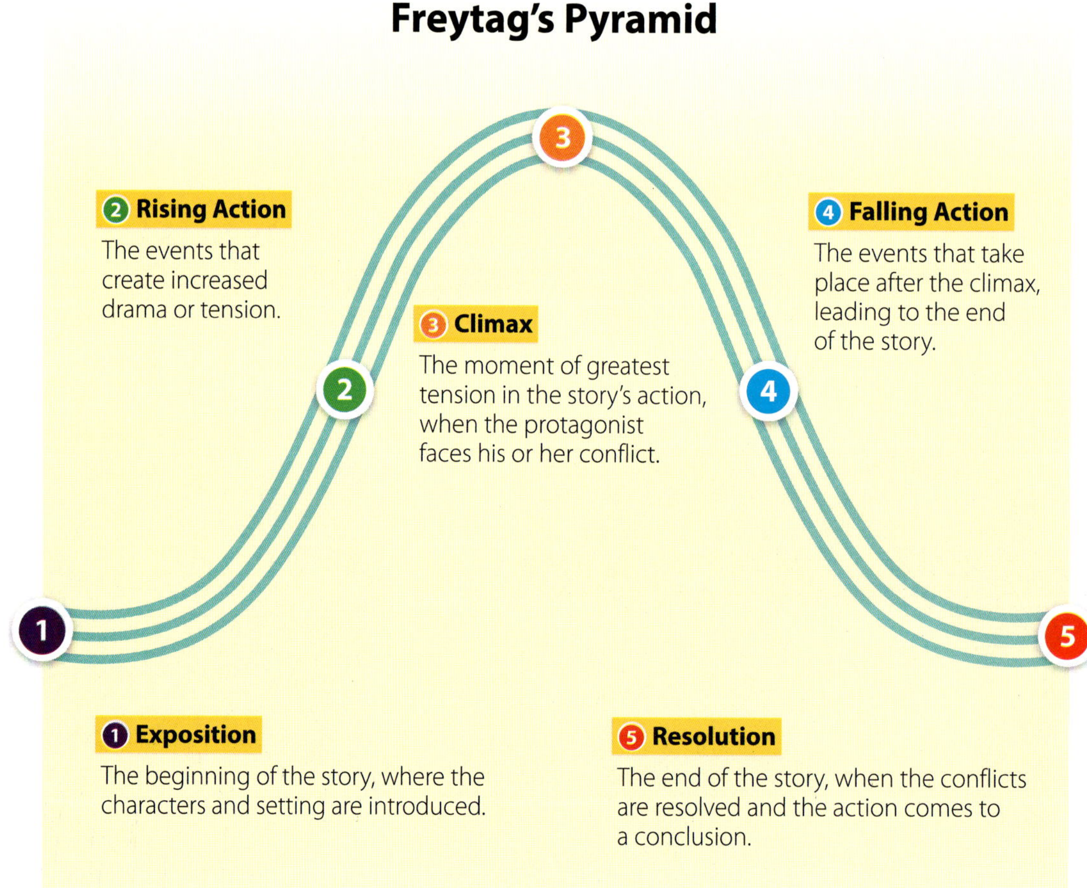

Plot

Plot is a word that describes the way a story's events unfold and fit together. It is the sequence of events that drive the characters toward the conclusion. While *The Kite Runner* occasionally deviates from a chronological sequence, Amir generally tells the story in the order in which the events happened.

Plot Points in Chapter five of *The Kite Runner*

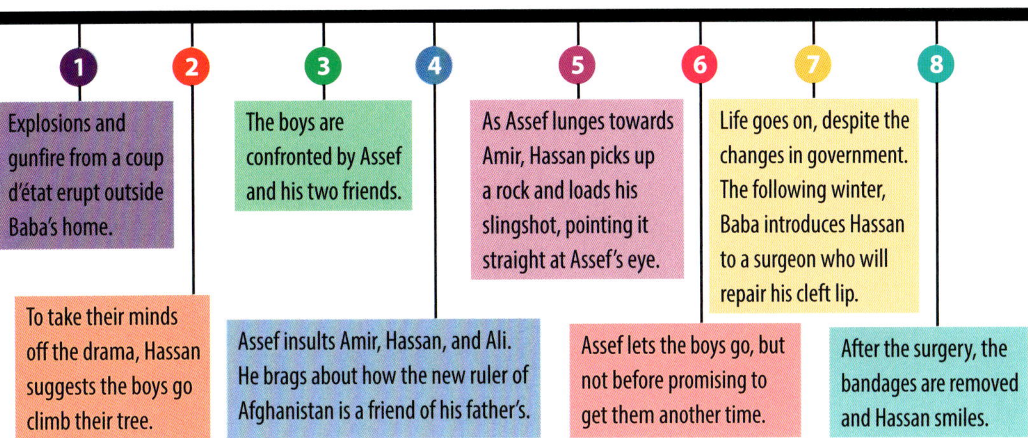

Literary Devices

Stories that employ literary devices cause readers to question, analyze, and delve deeper to find hidden, or less obvious meanings and lessons. Using these elements and techniques in a story allows an author to connect with readers by making them invest their emotions and beliefs in the story.

ACTIVITIES

Weblink

Khaled Hosseini: How I Write
Examine some of Hosseini's reflections about writing.

1. Hosseini explains how *The Kite Runner* began as a "short story, which was about 25 pages long." It was only after rereading it a couple of years later that he decided to expand it into a longer work. How might the short story format have limited its potential? Justify your answers with examples from the novel.
2. According to Hosseini, he was initially opposed to his wife's suggestion that he publish the manuscript, assuming that "no one in the U.S. would want to hear from an Afghan." How might the political climate at the time have contributed to this belief? In what ways did the eventual publication of the novel help to correct "misconceptions and preconceived notions about Afghanistan"?

More

Examples of Literary Techniques from the Novel
Analyze the author's use of literary techniques and how they contribute to the narrative of *The Kite Runner.*

1. Choose one literary technique used in the novel. In what particular way did the author use this literary technique? How effective was its usage?
2. What arguments can be made for the use of your chosen literary technique in a text? If this technique were overused or underutilized, what effect might it have on an author's work?

Theme in the Novel

To an author, a story's theme is like an explorer's compass—it keeps the story going in the right direction. The theme is the meaning of the story. Stories such as *The Kite Runner*, which span long time periods, stretch across countries and continents, and feature multiple characters, often explore several themes. As characters move through space and time, they encounter questions, ideas, problems, and challenges. These encounters force the characters to think, speak, and act in ways that relate back to the themes of the story. Authors revisit themes throughout a story to show how characters learn, change, and grow.

Values

The themes in a story reveal the mindset, ideas, thoughts, values, and desires not only of the characters, but of the author as well. An author's values often act as the base of the story. Without these values and the desire to share them, the idea for a story may never occur. While not all stories are autobiographical, they can nonetheless give a reader some insight into the author's personal values.

Major Themes of *The Kite Runner*

Hosseini opens *The Kite Runner* by exploring some of the major themes, and by revealing an important lesson the protagonist will come to learn. The author lays the foundation of the story, setting the stage for his exploration of themes such as the past, redemption, and how relationships evolve through time. With these opening thoughts, the author has placed them in the mind of the reader, giving clear direction to the story.

The Past

"As I drove, I wondered why I was different. Maybe it was because I had been raised by men; I hadn't grown up around women and had never been exposed firsthand to the double standard with which Afghan society sometimes treated them. Maybe it was because Baba had been such an unusual Afghan father, a liberal who had lived by his own rules, a maverick who had disregarded or embraced societal customs as he had seen fit.
But I think a big part of the reason I didn't care about Soraya's past was that I had one of my own. I knew all about regret."

Amir, Chapter thirteen

Amir

Redemption

"Rahim Khan had wanted me to stay with him a few more days, to plan more thoroughly. But I knew I had to leave as soon as possible. I was afraid I'd change my mind. I was afraid I'd deliberate, ruminate, agonize, rationalize, and talk myself into not going. I was afraid the appeal of my life in America would draw me back, that I would wade back into that great, big river and let myself forget, let the things I had learned these last few days sink to the bottom. I was afraid that I'd let the waters carry me away from what I had to do. From Hassan. From the past that had come calling. And from this one last chance at redemption."

Amir, Chapter nineteen

Father/Son Relationship

"Here is another cliché my creative writing teacher would have scoffed at; like father, like son. But it was true, wasn't it? As it turned out, Baba and I were more alike than I'd ever known. We had both betrayed the people who would have given their lives for us. And with that came this realization: that Rahim Khan had summoned me here to atone not just for my sins but for Baba's too."

Amir, Chapter eighteen

Amir

Secondary Themes

While books such as *The Kite Runner* feature obvious major themes, they often also touch on other, secondary themes. In *The Kite Runner*, secondary themes of innocence, guilt, and loyalty help to support the major themes by adding depth and encouraging further analysis by readers.

ACTIVITIES

Weblink

A HANDY GUIDE TO THE MOST COMMON THEMES IN LITERATURE

Evaluate the article from The Writers Academy discussing theme.

1. *The Kite Runner* is listed as a famous example of a "coming of age" story, in which "the character is forever changed...or achieves significant personal growth." Do you think this is an accurate assessment of Amir's journey? Explain in your own words how he has changed by the end of the novel. How does this exemplify significant personal growth?
2. According to the writer of the article, "a moral can be a theme, but a theme doesn't have to be a moral." How does this statement apply to *The Kite Runner*? Provide specific examples from the text.

More

Major and Secondary Themes

Analyze the author's development of themes over the course of the novel.

1. Choose a secondary theme from this spread and analyze its appearances in the novel. How does this theme first emerge? Which is the most poignant example of this theme in the novel?
2. What particular commentary might the author be making about life as a result of this theme's presence in the text? Explain and defend your ideas.
3. Choose a major theme presented on pages 16–17. In what ways does your chosen secondary theme relate to this major theme? Does it deepen or detract from the major theme? How or in what way?

RUBRIC

Creating a Symbolism Poster

Students will choose one of the other symbols listed on page 19 and analyze its role in the novel. They will then create a poster to present their analysis. An exemplary symbolism poster will meet the following criteria.

- Presents a clear purpose that is conveyed throughout the poster
- Shows an understanding of the concept of symbolism and the role it has in the novel
- Provides an in-depth analysis of what the symbol represents
- Discusses the role the symbol has in the novel
- Clearly indicates where the symbol appears in the novel
- Uses specific, detailed examples from the text to support the analysis
- Makes clear connections to the text
- Properly integrates all quotations
- Organizes the information in a logical, easy-to-read manner
- Includes high-quality graphics that relate to the symbol and effectively enhance understanding of the topic
- Features clear and concise writing
- Uses correct spelling, grammar, and punctuation
- Clearly labels items of importance
- Headings and subheadings are clear and easy to read
- Uses layout to creatively enhances the information
- Creates a poster that is attractive in terms of layout, design, and organization
- Shows a strong effort by the student

Symbolism in the Novel

Symbols give meaning to themes and occurrences in a story. An author uses symbolism to reveal themes through imagery and analysis. Using symbolism, an author leads the reader to form conclusions and understand themes. Symbols create a more immersive reading experience by engaging a reader's imagination, leading to a deeper connection between the reader and the story.

Hosseini uses symbolism throughout *The Kite Runner* so the reader further understands the characters and the unique cultural aspects of the story. Symbols such as Baba's legendary fight against a black bear and Hassan's dream about a monster in the lake help to reveal Amir's deepest fears, doubts, and regrets. Scenes unfolding around the pomegranate tree near Baba's house add an element of understanding to the evolution of Amir, his relationship with Hassan, and the devastation of war. Kite fighting and the flying of kites are symbols that recur throughout the story, demonstrating Amir's freedom, happiness, and eventual redemption.

The Cleft Lip as a Symbol

The cleft lip is a significant feature, not only on Hassan's face, but in Amir's and Baba's hearts and minds. When Baba pays to have Hassan's lip surgically repaired, it is supposed to "fix" Hassan's smile permanently. Readers later discover it was also an attempt to make up for Baba's own transgressions. However, the smile disappears forever from Hassan's face. The gift of surgery from Baba creates a sense of equality between Hassan and Amir. This adds to the jealousy Amir feels in regards to Hassan's relationship with Baba, compared to his own. Later, Amir's lip requires emergency surgery, linking him back to Hassan on a physical level. The matching scar is a symbol of Hassan that Amir will carry with him for the rest of his life.

Cleft Lip

"Later, after Aisha changed the IV tubing and raised the head of the bed like I'd asked, I thought about what had happened to me. Ruptured spleen. Broken teeth. Punctured lung. Busted eye socket. But as I watched a pigeon peck at a bread crumb on the windowsill, I kept thinking of something else Armand/Dr. Faruqi had said: *The impact had cut your upper lip in two,* he had said, *clean down the middle.* Clean down the middle. Like a harelip."

Amir, Chapter twenty-three

Amir

Who is connected to the cleft lip?

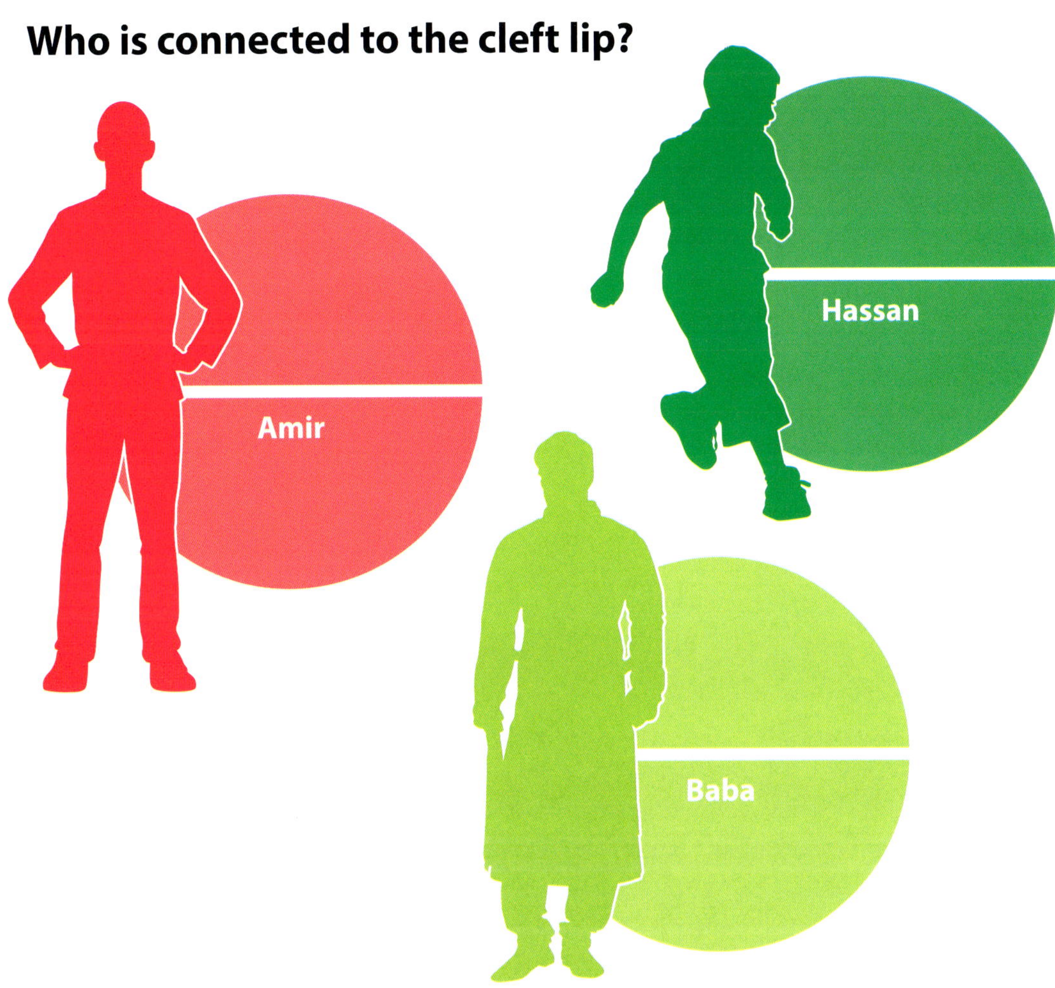

Other Symbols in the Novel

Baba's House

Baba's house in Kabul symbolizes the hopes and dreams, not only of Baba and Amir, but of millions of Afghans as well. In the early chapters of the novel, it is described as being one of the finest, most beautiful homes in all of Kabul. However, when Amir later returns to his war-torn hometown, the house is crumbling and seems much smaller than he remembers it.

Slingshot

Twice in the story, Amir is saved from Assef by a slingshot. The slingshot is a symbol that is often used in literature to invoke the biblical story of David and Goliath, in which David, against all odds, defeats the giant, Goliath. Hassan first saves Amir by threatening Assef with his slingshot, and later, Sohrab is forced to carry out what his father had threatened many years before, by shooting Assef in the eye to save Amir.

ACTIVITIES

 **More**

What Symbols Appear in the Novel?
Assess the author's use of symbolism in the novel.

1. Choose a character from the chart and analyze what the symbol of the cleft lip represents to him. For which character is this symbol the most poignant in the novel? For which character is the symbol least poignant? Argue your opinions with clear reasons.
2. How is this symbol used or reflected in the novel's themes? Illustrate the ways in which the author's use of language deepens or weakens the meaning of the cleft lip as a symbol. Explain and defend your ideas.

Weblink

The Complete Guide to Symbolism
Examine the blog post discussing the usage of symbolism in literature.

1. Contrast and compare examples of analytical descriptions of feelings and sensory descriptions using symbolism from the novel. Which kind is more effective in the novel? Provide reasons for your ideas.
2. Should analytical descriptions play a considerable role in the language of a novel? Why or why not?

The Use of Language

Language plays a key role in describing and relating the cultures at play in *The Kite Runner*. As an Afghan immigrant to the United States, Hosseini strives to create an understanding of how the two cultures can exist in one person. Throughout the story, the author blends words and phrases from his native tongue into English sentences and explanations. This technique helps remind readers of the importance of Afghan culture in the story, and also creates a level of understanding. Explaining situations, practices, and beliefs using the Farsi or Arabic words gives English-speaking readers a more in-depth cultural experience. Reading words in the protagonist's and author's native language also makes it easier to imagine and understand the lives they have lead, and the struggles they have overcome.

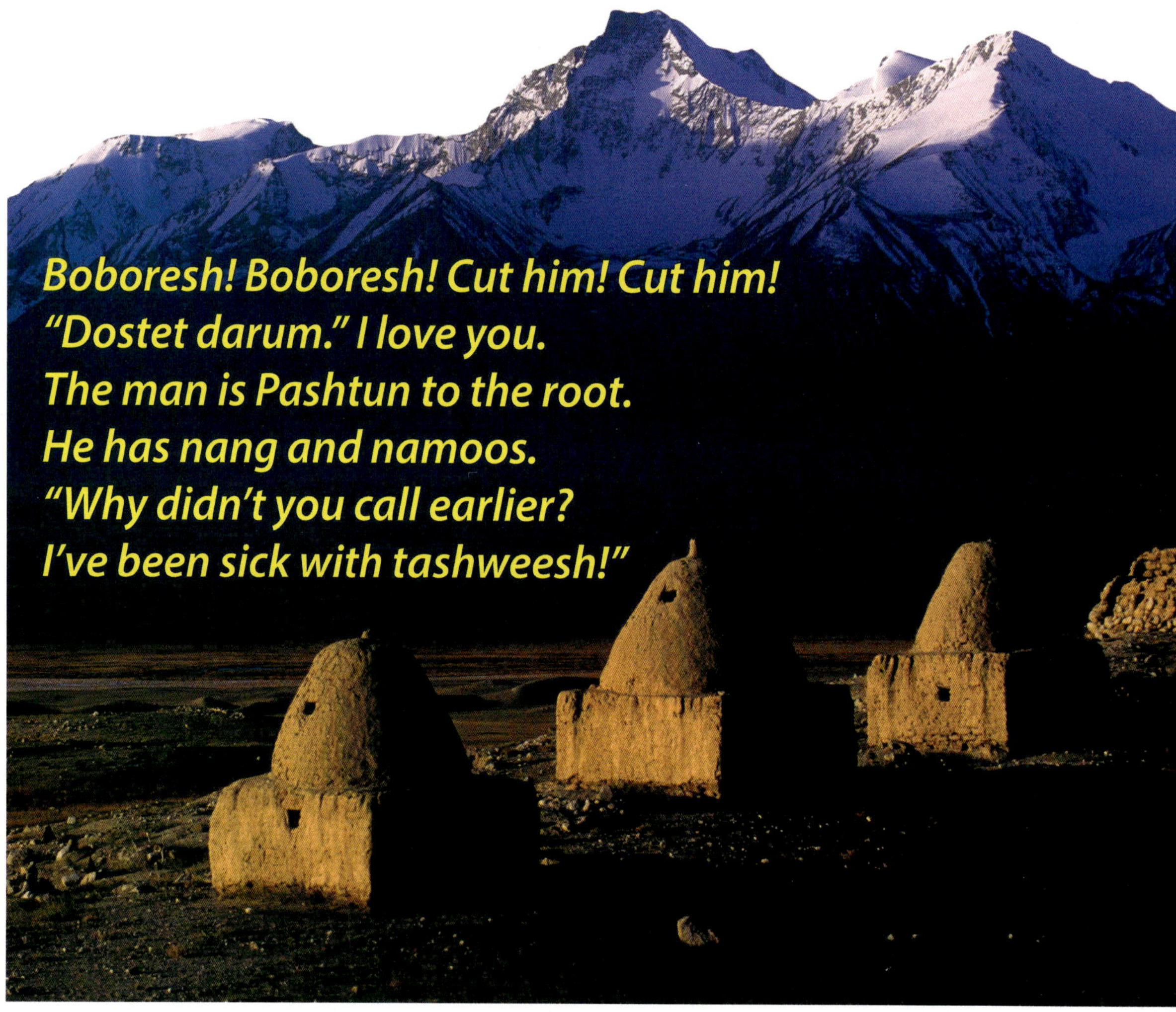

Culture

Cultural differences are manifested in many ways throughout *The Kite Runner*. While Amir and Hassan are both born and raised together in Kabul, they come from different cultural backgrounds, which is clearly demonstrated in the way the two boys speak. Hassan always speaks to Amir respectfully, often in **reverence**. Phrases such as, "for you, a thousand times over," reflect Hassan's respectful, loving nature, but also his subservient status as a Hazara. Amir, on the other hand, is often disrespectful to Hassan in his language, manipulating stories to fool the illiterate Hassan, demonstrating the clear cultural gap between them.

A Little Trick

"One day, in July 1973, I played another little trick on Hassan. I was reading to him, and suddenly I strayed from the written story. I pretended I was reading from the book, flipping pages regularly, but I had abandoned the text altogether, taken over the story, and made up my own. Hassan, of course, was oblivious to this. To him, the words on the page were a scramble of codes, indecipherable, mysterious. Words were secret doorways and I held all the keys. After, I started to ask him if he'd liked the story, a giggle rising in my throat, when Hassan began to clap.

'What are you doing?' I said.

'That was the best story you've read me in a long time,' he said, still clapping."

Amir, Chapter four

Amir

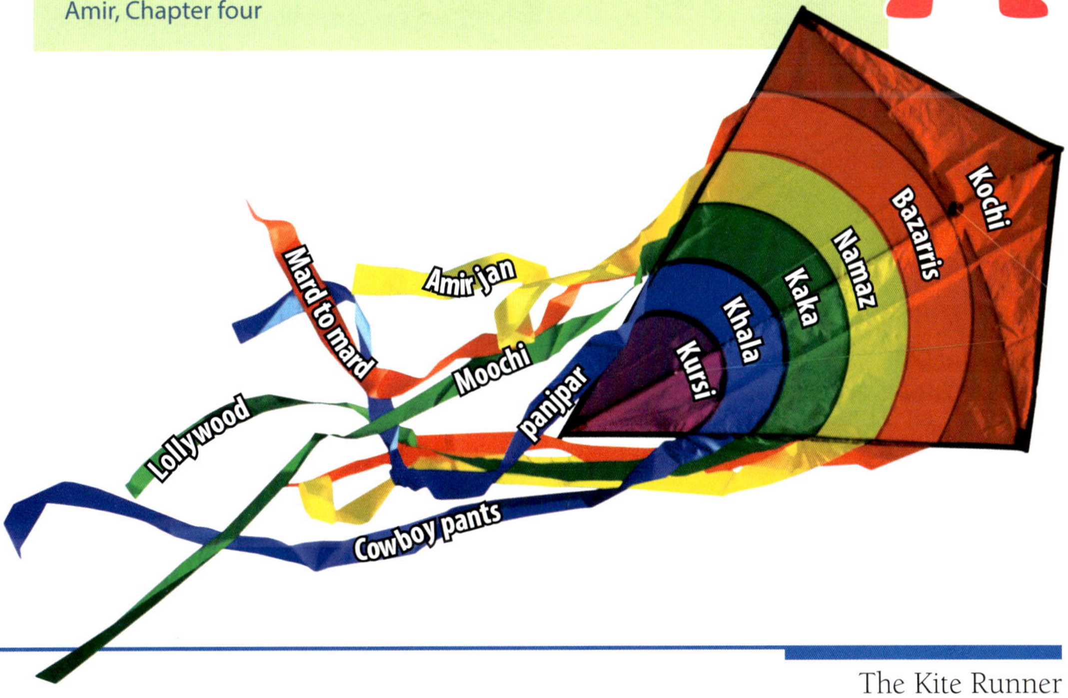

Kochi
Bazarris
Namaz
Kaka
Khala
Kursi
panjpar
Moochi
Amir jan
Mard to mard
Lollywood
Cowboy pants

ACTIVITIES

Document

The Role of Linguistic Devices in Representing Ethnicity in The Kite Runner

Analyze the publication by Asghar Malik, Syed Kazim Shah, and Rashid Mahmood, analyzing the linguistic devices used in the novel.

1. Which linguistic devices are examined in the study? How does Hosseini use them, and to what effect? Give specific examples.
2. The study attempts to determine how Hosseini "manipulate[s] the text of the novel to represent ethnicity." Do you think it is fair to say that Hosseini has "manipulated" the text? If so, explain how he has done this, citing evidence from the novel. If not, defend your position.

Weblink

PEOPLE HERE, PEOPLE THERE

Find out more about the cultural differences between Afghanistan and America by reading the article by Ab Majeed Dar.

1. The writer claims that "In Afghanistan, there is a strong focus on male to male relationships." How is this exemplified in *The Kite Runner*? In what ways do such male to male relationships differ from male to female relationships, such as the one between Amir and Soraya? What accounts for these differences?
2. The writer says that "The cultural differences between America and Afghanistan...are best seen in the types of relationships the protagonist, Amir, makes with those around him." Do you agree with this assertion? Explain why or why not.

RUBRIC

Writing a Review

Students will write a review of the novel. An exemplary review will meet the following criteria.

- Grabs the reader's attention with a creative headline
- Begins with an engaging lead to pull the reader into the article
- Introduces the title of the novel, the author, and the genre
- Provides a brief plot description that does not give away the entire story, and makes the reader want to learn more about the novel
- Supports arguments about the novel with accurate and detailed information
- Organizes the review and its arguments in a concise, clear, and logical manner
- Fits the format and style of a review
- Follows the conventions of print or online journalism
- Demonstrates creativity in their approach
- Writes with a unique, engaging voice and perspective
- Provides fresh insight into the novel
- Provides an honest, authentic opinion on the novel
- Gives a clear recommendation on the novel, backed up by specific textual evidence
- Uses correct spelling, grammar, and punctuation

Impact of the Novel at the Time of Publishing

The Kite Runner was published at a tumultuous time between America and Afghanistan. The U.S. military had recently invaded Afghanistan, following the attacks of September 11, 2001. Afghanistan was a popular and controversial topic of conversation, and often appeared in the news. *The Kite Runner* also came with its share of controversy along with success.

Publication

Hosseini learned quickly that writing a book is not necessarily the same as being a published author. After he finished writing *The Kite Runner*, Hosseini began sending the story to **literary agents**, hoping someone could sell his novel to a publisher. Before he found representation and publication, Hosseini's manuscript was rejected by more than 20 agents.

Criticism

Each agent had his or her own reasons for rejecting Hosseini's book. After its publication, *The Kite Runner* found many more critics among readers and reviewers. A 2003 review in Britain's *The Guardian* newspaper called *The Kite Runner*, "an unconvincing **melodrama**, more concerned with packing in the action than with fictional integrity." Other reviewers, however, were much more positive. *The New York Times* called *The Kite Runner*, "[a] powerful first novel," and, "[a] vivid and engaging story."

Graphic Scenes

While some literary critics may not have liked Hosseini's writing style or his storytelling techniques, many members of the general public focused negatively on one particular aspect of the book. The scene in which Hassan is assaulted in chapter seven is shocking, memorable, and moving. Many readers and potential readers found it to be too shocking and graphic, especially for certain age groups. Hosseini has defended the scene as "pivotal," and claims that, "Without it the story falls apart." He has also called the scene "metaphoric," stating that, "a lot of fellow Afghans feel like that's what happened to their country."

In 2007, *The Kite Runner* was adapted as a film. It was originally praised for casting Afghan actors to portray the main characters. However, as word of the controversial assault scene spread, threats were made, and the film's release was delayed while the actors were moved out of Afghanistan for their own safety. Upon its release, the film was nominated for several major awards, including two Golden Globes and an Academy Award.

In **2004**, *The Kite Runner* became one of the **top 50** bestsellers. For the next four years, it would rise to the **top ten bestsellers** worldwide.

The Kite Runner spent **more than 100 weeks** on *The New York Times* **bestseller list**.

Around the world, the **film adaptation** of *The Kite Runner* made **$73 million**.

ACTIVITIES

Document

From harelip to split lip

Analyze the review by Sarah A. Smith, published on October 4, 2003, exploring her views on *The Kite Runner*.

1. What is the tone of the review? Do you agree with Smith's assessment of the novel? Why or why not?
2. According to Smith, "a few too many parallels let down... *The Kite Runner*." Do you think this is true? Defend your opinion with solid arguments and cite passages from the novel as evidence.

Weblink

The Kite Runner

Find out more about the film adaptation's critical reception in this review by Roger Ebert, published on December 13, 2007.

1. Ebert says that the film "superimposes human faces and a historical context on the tragic images of war from Afghanistan." Is this true of the novel as well? Explain why you think so.
2. Ebert believes that the film "sidesteps the emotional disconnects we often feel when a story moves between past and present." Is this a potential risk in other forms of storytelling? Do you think this is done successfully in the novel? Why or why not?

RUBRIC

Analyzing a Video

Students will watch and assess a video related to a component of the novel, and write an analysis of the video. An exemplary video analysis will meet the following criteria.

- Identifies the purpose of the video
- Identifies the intended audience of the video
- Describes how the content of the video is presented
- Summarizes the information and opinions presented in the video
- Analyzes the quality of the content presented in the video
- Assesses the effectiveness of the video
- Discusses the technical aspects of the video and whether or not these enhance the content
- Determines whether the images and graphics used in the video relate to the content
- Determines whether the video is easy to follow and understand
- Gives the analysis a clear and consistent purpose
- Organizes the analysis in a logical, effective manner
- Presents a strong, clear argument about the video
- Provides strong and accurate details to support the argument about the video
- Considers other perspectives on the purpose and effectiveness of the video
- Makes connections between the video and the novel
- Properly integrates quotations from the video
- Cites all sources used in the analysis

Impact of the Novel Now

Since it was first published, *The Kite Runner* has become what many critics consider a modern classic. It has sold millions of copies around the world, and has helped make its author, an Afghan refugee, one of America's most beloved twenty-first century writers. *The Kite Runner* has been taught as part of high school curricula across America and around the world. Its sensitive subject matter and relatable characters have raised understanding and awareness of the struggles faced by many refugees and victims of war, in Afghanistan and elsewhere.

Awards and Sales

By the time *The Kite Runner* movie was released in 2007, more than four million copies of the novel had been sold. The book also won several major awards, including Best Book of 2003 from the *San Francisco Chronicle* and *Entertainment Weekly*. Since then, other major accolades have followed. In 2012, *The Kite Runner* was chosen as a title to read for the first World Book Day held in the United States.

To date, more than **31.5 million** copies of *The Kite Runner* have been sold **around the world**.

60 *The Kite Runner* has been translated into **more than 60** languages.

The **UNHCR** estimates that there are about **22.5 million** refugees around the world.

More Adaptations

In 2012, Hosseini, a fan of comic books and graphic novels, agreed to work with visual artists Fabio Celoni and Mirka Andolfo. They illustrated Amir's story for *The Kite Runner* graphic novel. The idea was to make the story accessible to a wider audience. Another adaptation has delivered Hosseini's story to live audiences. *The Kite Runner* play first appeared on stage in San Jose in 2009, earning mixed reviews from audiences and critics. A production was later staged in the United Kingdom, in 2013. This version was much more celebrated, moving from the Nottingham Playhouse to London's historic Wyndham's Theatre.

Censorship and Challenges

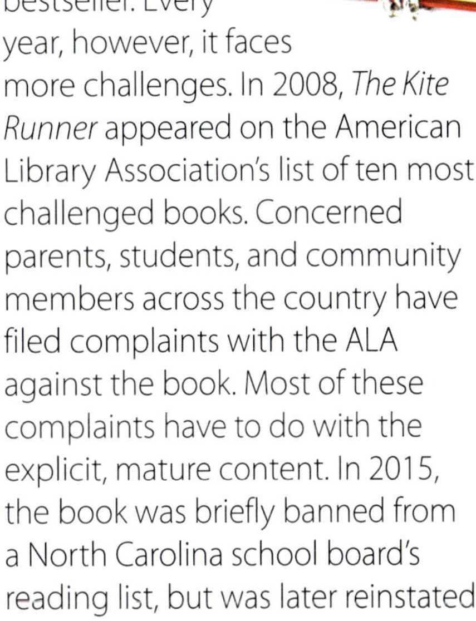

The Kite Runner has overcome much criticism, growing from a rejected short story into an international bestseller. Every year, however, it faces more challenges. In 2008, *The Kite Runner* appeared on the American Library Association's list of ten most challenged books. Concerned parents, students, and community members across the country have filed complaints with the ALA against the book. Most of these complaints have to do with the explicit, mature content. In 2015, the book was briefly banned from a North Carolina school board's reading list, but was later reinstated.

Hosseini Foundation

The success Hosseini found with his debut novel not only changed his life, but allowed him to impact others' lives as well. *The Kite Runner* propelled Hosseini into the public spotlight, giving him the opportunity to help people. After a 2007 trip to Afghanistan with the UNHCR, Hosseini decided to give back to his homeland. Along with his wife, he created the Khaled Hosseini Foundation, which raises funding and awareness to supply Afghan women, children, and refugees with resources such as shelter, health care, and education.

ACTIVITIES

Video

A conversation with Khaled Hosseini

Learn more about Hosseini and his foundation by watching this video.

1. In the video, Hosseini says that the characters in his books live through the upheavals of the last 40 years, and that his foundation is "an attempt to access and reach real-life people who are the counterparts of those characters." What does he mean by this? How does knowing that such real-life counterparts exist affect your interpretation of the fictional characters in the novel?
2. Hosseini points out that he is a former refugee himself. How important is this for telling this particular story? What might be different if this kind of story were written by someone without personal experience as a refugee?

Document

'The Kite Runner': Theater Review

Analyze the review by Stephen Dalton, published on January 11, 2017, analyzing the theatrical adaptation of *The Kite Runner*.

1. Dalton claims that "Croft's production lacks...the textured detail of the novel." What do you think he means by this? Would you describe the novel as being particularly detailed? Why?
2. In Dalton's opinion, the motivations of the characters in the play are "mostly reducible to a single personality trait." Do you think this is the case in the novel or are its characters more complex? Which personality trait best defines Amir's motivation? Is this his only motivation? Explain your answer.

RUBRIC

Creating a Timeline

Students will explore a topic related to the novel and create a timeline to present their research on historical events connected to this topic. An exemplary timeline will meet the following criteria.

- Includes the most significant events pertaining to the topic to be compared and analyzed
- Includes interesting events
- Uses accurate information for all events, including date, location, and major details
- Orders the events in a chronological sequence
- Describes each event with accurate, vivid, and specific details
- Presents the topic from three or more perspectives
- Inspires the reader to ask thoughtful questions regarding the events and perspectives presented in the timeline
- Uses correct spelling, grammar, and punctuation
- Presents the timeline in a visually attractive and striking manner
- Presents the timeline in a neat, organized manner that is logical and easy to follow
- Uses creativity to present the timeline in an engaging manner
- Effectively communicates the historical information relating to the topic
- Supports each event with reliable sources
- Expresses a clear purpose for creating the timeline
- Enhances the reader's understanding of the topic
- Includes a correctly formatted bibliography of all sources used to create the timeline

Perspectives on Refugees

As a refugee who was granted **political asylum** in the United States, received a high-level education, and became a successful author, Hosseini could be considered lucky. Many other Afghans have been killed, and although millions more have escaped, they have often gone on to live difficult lives in their new countries. However, despite his successes, Hosseini's life in the United States has also had its struggles, some of which are reflected in his semi-autobiographical debut novel.

Afghanistan Refugee Crisis Timeline

1900s

1933 Zahir Shah becomes Afghanistan's King.

1973 General Mohammed Daud launches a military coup, seizing power from the King.

1978 In another coup, Daud is killed, and a Soviet-backed government takes control.

1979 After opposition from **mujahideen** groups, supported by the United States, the Soviet Union invades Afghanistan, keeping communists in power. Weapons supplied by countries such as the U.S., China, Pakistan, and Saudi Arabia, are sent to the mujahideen in order to fight the Soviets.

1985 As fighting continues, half of Afghanistan's population is believed to be displaced by the war.

The Kite Runner gives readers a glimpse into the mind of a refugee and everything he was forced to leave behind. While Amir is granted a chance at a new beginning in the United States, he is haunted by his past in Afghanistan. He tries his best to move on, and to leave his memories and torment behind. When he receives a phone call from Rahim Khan, however, Amir's past, and the ghosts of Afghanistan, call him home. Amir's longing for redemption, his guilt, and his desire to be set free despite his freedom are emotions shared by many refugees. Like Amir, Hosseini found reconciliation by revisiting his past in Afghanistan.

1988 A peace accord is signed, and the Soviet Union withdraws from Afghanistan. Civil war continues, however, as mujahideen groups fight for control.

1998 The United States fires missiles at Afghanistan bases suspected of sheltering the terrorist Osama bin Laden. He was wanted for bombing American embassies in Africa, and was being protected by the Taliban.

2000s

1996 The Taliban takes control of Kabul, creating a fundamentalist Islamic government. In the continuing civil war, the Taliban would spread its control throughout the country.

2014 The UNHCR announces that Afghanistan has produced the world's highest number of refugees for more than three decades. That year, 2.6 million Afghans are displaced from their homes.

2001 After the September 11 attack on the United States, the U.S. military bombs Afghanistan. The U.S.-led invasion takes power away from the Taliban, and Hamid Karzai becomes president. Fierce fighting, however, continues.

ACTIVITIES

Transparency–Timeline

Afghanistan Refugee Crisis Timeline

Examine the historical and cultural contexts shown on the timeline. Then, contrast and correlate its elements with the themes and events presented in *The Kite Runner.*

1. In what ways can historical events, culture, and social mores influence a population's perspective on refugees? How might these elements have shaped the way a reader in the early 2000s interpreted the novel?
2. How might the era in which Khaled Hosseini wrote *The Kite Runner* have influenced the novel's themes and settings? Where in the novel is this most evident? Explain your reasoning.
3. Which current events, changes in laws, new ideas, or political discussions are shaping the refugee crisis in Afghanistan today? Which ideas and attitudes are still prevailing? Why?
4. How might current events and present perspectives affect the way a reader interprets the novel? Why is it important for readers to understand the era and context in which a novel is written?

RUBRIC

Writing a Comparative Essay

Students will compare two literary devices used in the novel, and then write a comparative essay based on their analysis. An exemplary comparative essay will meet the following criteria.

- Consists of a one-paragraph introduction, three body paragraphs, and a one-paragraph conclusion
- Introduction includes an engaging lead statement about the topic of the essay, more detailed information about the novel, and a one-sentence thesis that specifically states the essay's argument
- Body paragraphs include a topic sentence that refers to the thesis and how the idea appears in the novel, a supporting sentence that points to this part of the novel, textual evidence of this idea from the novel, and analysis of this evidence
- Body paragraphs end with a transition to the next paragraph
- Conclusion refers to the topic of the essay and the three points presented in the body paragraphs, and restates the thesis
- Provides a thorough analysis of the literary devices in question
- Cites strong and thorough textual evidence to support analysis of what the novel says explicitly
- Presents a clear, specific thesis that indicates a high level of critical engagement
- Organizes ideas in a logical manner
- Communicates arguments in a clear, effective manner
- Properly integrates all quotations
- Correctly cites all sources used
- Correctly formats bibliography

Writing a Comparative Essay

Some of the characters in *The Kite Runner* portray complex personalities and the ability to change. Others are more one-dimensional, symbolizing certain aspects of humanity as inherent. Choose two characters from the story, and list their traits and attributes. Compare the two characters and note how their attributes are similar or different. Write an essay explaining what makes the two characters unique, and in what ways they are similar. Support your argument using examples from the novel.

How to Analyze and Compare Characters

Use the chart to guide your comparison of two characters in *The Kite Runner*.

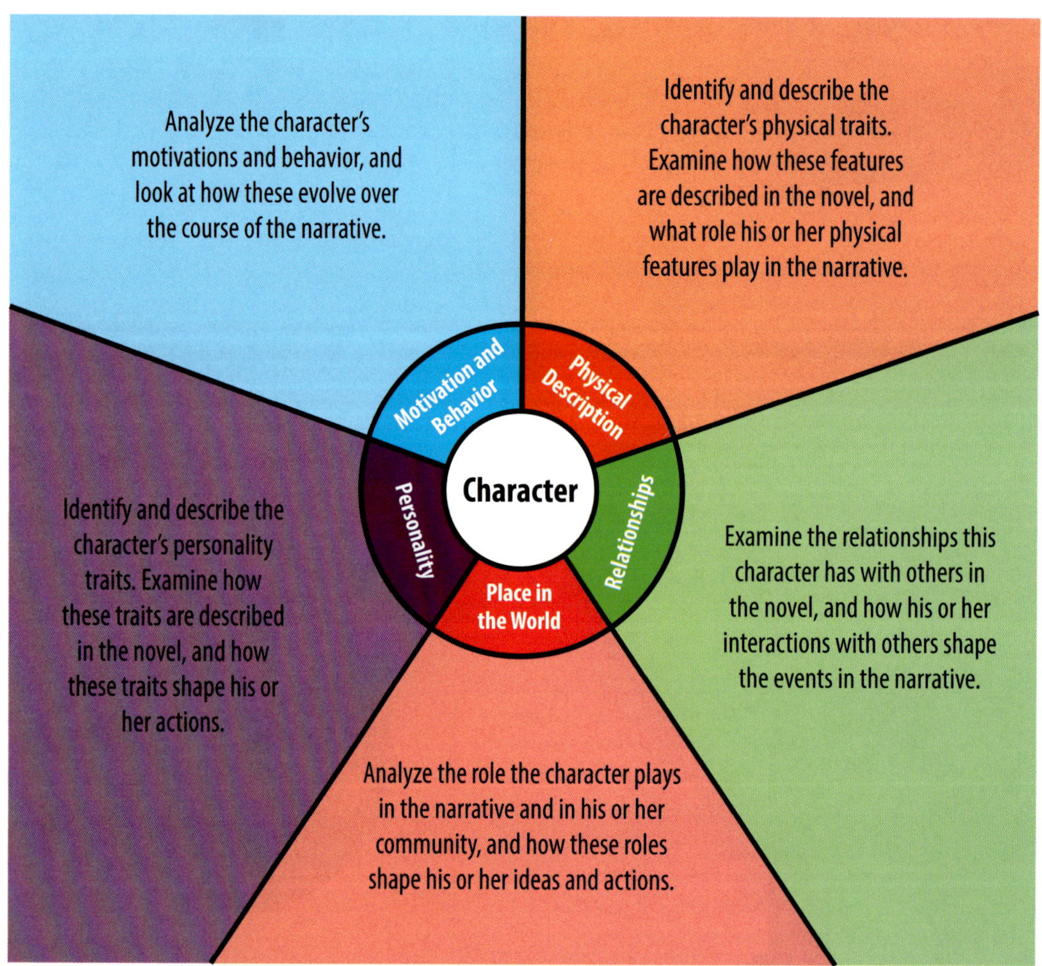

ACTIVITIES

Comparing Amir and Hassan

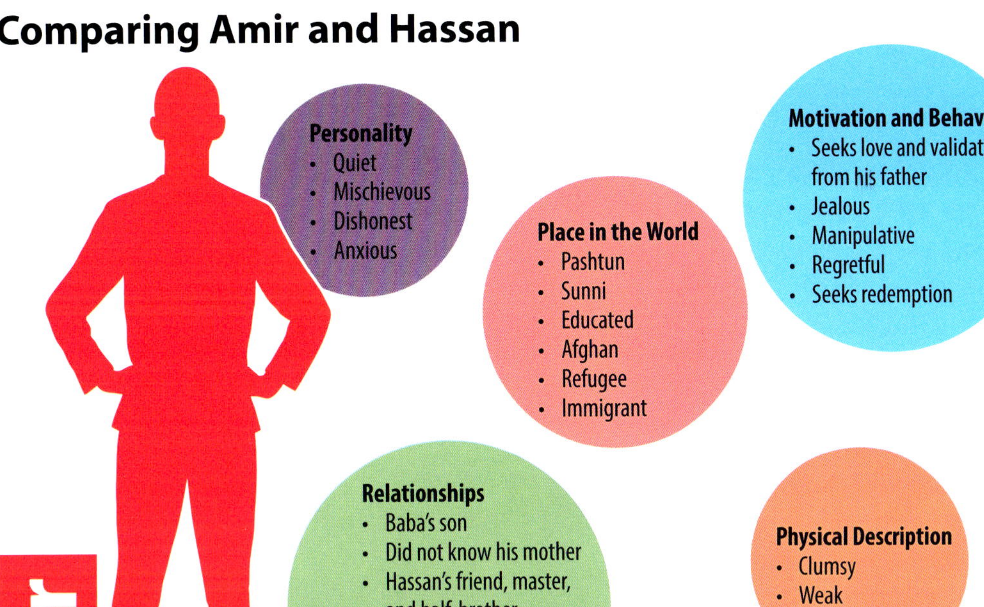

Amir

Personality
- Quiet
- Mischievous
- Dishonest
- Anxious

Place in the World
- Pashtun
- Sunni
- Educated
- Afghan
- Refugee
- Immigrant

Motivation and Behavior
- Seeks love and validation from his father
- Jealous
- Manipulative
- Regretful
- Seeks redemption

Relationships
- Baba's son
- Did not know his mother
- Hassan's friend, master, and half-brother
- Bullied by Assef
- Soraya's husband
- Sohrab's uncle

Physical Description
- Clumsy
- Weak

Hassan

Place in the World
- Hazara
- Shi'a
- Servant
- Illiterate
- Afghan

Physical Description
- Harelipped
- Almost perfectly round face
- Flat, broad nose
- Slanting, narrow eyes
- Tiny, low-set ears
- Pointed stub of a chin

Motivation and Behavior
- Loyal
- Protective
- Gentle
- Always smiling
- Strives to survive

Relationships
- Ali's son
- Baba's illegitimate son
- Did not know his mother
- Amir's best friend, servant, and half-brother
- Sohrab's father

Personality
- Honest
- Quiet
- Loyal
- Confident

More

Questions for Character Analysis

Analyze how specific character features, such as conflicts, motivations, relationships, place in the world, and personality affect the plot of *The Kite Runner*. Cite strong and thorough textual evidence to support your analysis of what the novel says explicitly as well as the inferences you may have drawn from the novel's setting, themes, and symbols.

Quiz Answers

1. B
2. D
3. B
4. C
5. A
6. C
7. B
8. D
9. B
10. B

Key Words

chronological: unfolding in a sequence along a timeline

coup: the overthrow of a government

diaspora: a particular population living outside its homeland

diplomat: a government worker whose job is to maintain relations with other countries

factions: individual groups that form within a larger group

Farsi: the official Iranian language spoken in Iran and parts of Afghanistan

fundamentalism: a system of beliefs that interprets religious texts literally

introspective: looking within

literary agents: people who work for authors, promoting and selling their work

melodrama: exaggerated emotion

mujahideen: Muslim guerrilla fighters

non-profit: an organization that does not earn profits for its work

political asylum: the act of accepting people into a country who would be in danger in their homeland, due to political circumstances

prognosis: the probable outcome of an illness

psyche: a person's soul, spirit, or mindset

reckoning: when a person is held accountable for his or her actions or deeds

reverence: an attitude of deep respect

sabbatical: a time period granted away from work

secularism: non-religiousness

terminal: in medicine, an illness that will end in death

Literary Terms

antagonist: the opposing force to the hero of the story

autobiographical: having to do with the author, and his or her life and experiences

character traits: aspects that make up a character's personality

dialogue: words spoken between characters

dynamic character: a character who changes throughout a story

imagery: a visual description

literary devices: unique structures of a literary work

literary elements: components of every literary work

mood: the feelings evoked by a story

motifs: major ideas in a literary work

narrative: a story

narrative structure: the way a story is built

protagonist: the hero of a story

static character: a character who does not display major personality changes

storyline: the plot of a story

tone: the attitude or feelings of a story conveyed through words or observations of a character

Index

LIGHTBOX

SUPPLEMENTARY RESOURCES

Click on the plus icon found in the bottom left corner of each spread to open additional teacher resources.

- Download and print the book's quizzes and activities
- Access curriculum correlations
- Explore additional web applications that enhance the Lightbox experience

LIGHTBOX DIGITAL TITLES

Packed full of integrated media

VIDEOS

INTERACTIVE MAPS

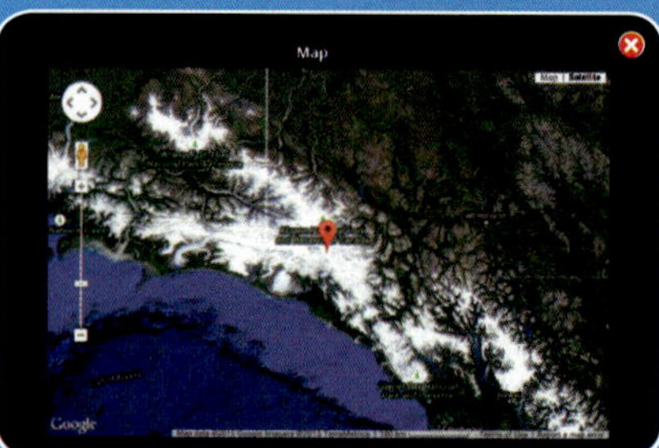

WEBLINKS

SLIDESHOWS

QUIZZES

OPTIMIZED FOR

- ✓ TABLETS
- ✓ WHITEBOARDS
- ✓ COMPUTERS
- ✓ AND MUCH MORE!

Published by Smartbook Media Inc.
350 5th Avenue, 59th Floor New York, NY 10118
Website: www.openlightbox.com

Library of Congress Cataloging-in-Publication Data
Names: Wiseman, Blaine, author. | Gillespie, Katie, author.
Title: The kite runner / Blaine Wiseman and Katie Gillespie.
Description: New York, NY : Smartbook Media Inc., 2018. | Series: Lightboxliterature studies | Includes index.
Identifiers: LCCN 2017054095 (print) | LCCN 2018004515 (ebook) | ISBN 9781510537118 (Multi-User eBook) | ISBN 9781510537101 (hard cover : alk.paper)
Subjects: LCSH: Hosseini, Khaled. Kite runner--History and criticism. | Hosseini, Khaled. Kite runner x Examinations--Study guides. | Kabul (Afghanistan) in literature. | Male friendship in literature. | Social classes in literature. | Betrayal in literature. | Boys in literature.
Classification: LCC PS3608.O832 (ebook) | LCC PS3608.O832 K5838 2018 (print)
| DDC 813/.6--dc23
LC record available at https://lccn.loc.gov/2017054095

Printed in Brainerd, Minnesota, United States
1 2 3 4 5 6 7 8 9 0 22 21 20 19 18

062018
121017

Editor: Katie Gillespie
Art Director: Terry Paulhus

The publisher acknowledges Getty Images, iStock, Alamy, Dreamstime, Shutterstock, and Wikipedia Commons as its primary image suppliers for this title.